out of the bones of earth

ALSO BY DEVREAUX BAKER

Red Willow People (Wild Ocean Press, 2011)
Beyond the Circumstance of Sight (Wild Ocean Press, 2009)
Light at the Edge (Pygmy Forest Press, 1993)

co-editor (with Sharon Doubiago and Susan Maeder),
Wood, Water, Air and Fire, The Anthology of Mendocino Women Poets (Pot Shard Press, 1998)

out of the bones of earth

poems

by

Devreaux Baker

Wild Ocean Press
San Francisco

Grateful acknowledgement to the following publications in which
several of these poems first appeared:

New Millennium Writings; ZYZZYVA;
Empirical; Crab Orchard Review; The Mas Tequila Review;
CUTTHROAT: A Journal Of The Arts;
and to
the Nuclear Age Peace Foundation ("In The Year Of The Drone"
awarded the 2014 Barbara Mandigo Kelley Poetry Peace Prize);
the Center for Women's Global Leadership ("My Name Means
Memory" awarded the 2012 Poetry Prize)

Library of Congress Cataloguing in Publication Data

Baker, Devreaux

out of the bones of earth / Devreaux Baker – 1ˢᵗ ed.

1. Title

ISBN: 978-1-941137-03-1

Cover design by Solange Roberdeau

Printed in the United States of America

Distributed by Small Press Distribution, Inc., Berkeley, CA
http://www.spdbooks.org

Wild Ocean Press
San Francisco, CA
www.wildoceanpress.com

to Barry

Contents

Letters From The New World

In the Year of the Drone

Basra Blues

You said if you could play Basra like a saxophone
it would be a long drawn out note from the belly of love
sent straight from the throat of the beginning of time
into the hereafter chambers of someone's idea
of a man-made hell.
There would be no room for the drumbeat of sorrow
to spin her own song about lost times
and compassion at the edges of sight
would disappear in a sandstorm
that blew fire for days.
You said you climbed into the hills on the other side of the city
just to blow some blue notes that could conjure the dead
after you held your best friend in your lap
and watched the nineteen years that made up his life
step out of his eyes and walk away from the left behind
shape of his body.
If forgiveness is a place each of us is capable of finding,
you search for those riffs that circle inside your head
and disappear before you have time to climb out of bed
and claim them as your own.
Basra comes etched with hieroglyphs of fear,
syllables urging you to watch each step you take
while you try to catch those chords
and transform them into a song.
Mornings you watched some men shoot dogs
while others wept and you kept trying to let go
of the shape of friends dying in your arms
or reflections of children in garbage-strewn puddles
that mark the streets they call home.
Basra Blues is a hymn that resonates in your chest
until you learn how to make a kind of peace
with the fractured face of war,
and hope whistles her own tune
in all the hills of your grief.

My Name Means Memory

*My name is Hafiza. I came from the East
during the war.* If you close your hands
over the tops of mine you can hear
nights unwrap themselves bent

with their burden
of broken wood or reaching deep
into frozen earth, fingers numb
with their own memories.

Wrap this memory like a shawl of dreams
around your shoulders. My husband carried
our youngest son ten days and nights
from our home to the camps

moving like a chant through fields
of frozen birds, crying when he broke
their wings beneath his feet.

Pain was the swelling around the dark fruit
we were forced to eat for bread. It was the wafer
that melted against our tongues causing us to carry
the dark seeds into our throats, rattling beneath our ribs

until they blossomed deep inside our bodies
and caused us to dream a pathway
for reunions with death time and again.
They are the flowers of witness that bloom even

when I try to forget. Carry this picture then
in your locket and wear it on a silver chain
next to your heart forever, as I wear it
softly swinging on a thread of memory,

swinging between my breasts like a prayer
repeating the same words over and over,
*my name is Hafiza. I came from the East
during the war.*

Dialect Of War

I never knew if you thought joining up
was an entrance way to some bright new beginning
or the slamming shut of some door
against everything you were
before you put the uniform on.

I remember your mother ironing your shirts,
the smell of steam unfolding stories in her kitchen,
how proud she was of you preparing to leave
for a destination she could not pronounce

Falluja   Kandahar   Islamabad

Later the sound of those names filled her body
with the weight of so much pain she knelt
in the middle of that floor, hands covered with flour
from bread rising on the counter just behind her.

None of us knew what your deployment would mean
with its abandoned territory of left behind words
we kept trying to navigate our way through.

When your letters arrived, fragile as friends
who died in your arms, we felt their ghosts
enter that hidden place at the base of our throats
where words wake up from sleep

and in that way we came to be filled with a dialect of war,
an alphabet of grief, syllables that represent
people and places we will never know
beyond the mute world of loss.

At night when we lay down to sleep, the names
Islamabad or *Kabul*
drift inside our mouths like a mantra for the disappeared,
entire families who once sat down to share bread
or celebrate birth.

Homecoming

Stepping off the plane sixty years later
you kept passing shadows etched into walls
with faces from the past.

There was the smell of cordite in the air
firewood tied in red bundles
on women's backs.

We followed the wrist bone of road
curving up and over fragile fields
like forgotten hands praying.

It carried fingerprints of fire
like gypsy lanterns waving
in a dream of ash and smoke.

I walked with you down cobblestones
searching through an archeology of rubble
for friends and family left behind.

All gone, all gone were words you whispered
until you saw the woman waving from her
bullet-riddled house.

Everything grew very still while wind in trees
cradled our bodies
in a spell of reconciliation.

It was a tapestry only childhood friends
once lost, now found
could weave together

lifelines blossoming and unfolding
into one hundred red petals
of homecoming.

In The Year Of The Drone

Hurry, you have to tell them.

A girl is walking down the street
hand in hand with her mother
coming or going to a wedding or a birth.
There is the sound of celebration in the air
the smell of spice on their hair and fingers.

You have to warn them.

The vendors are setting up carts
at the edges of the street.
A woman carries her baby in her arms,
a man lifts his son onto his shoulders
for a better view of our world.

Somewhere miles and lifetimes away
men sit in a room lit by screens,
dead light is trapped against their forms.
You know how this will end.

You have to warn them.

When Cortes burned the aviaries
he chose to destroy what was innocent,
what was precious to the people.
He chose to wage war by first putting to flame
Great Blue Herons, Snowy Egrets
Spring Tanagers and Hummingbirds.

You have to go now.

A burning coin has been tossed in the air.
There are faces lit by dead light
watching from miles and lifetimes away.

This Is Not My Empire

This is the night
that only ends when one person says   *Enough*
and passes on the words that sing solidarity
from heart to hand to mouth
so an unbreakable bond is formed,
a chain is forged
an empire is dismantled
so a new land grows up
out of the shadow world into the light
where even the voices of those whose language
we do not speak is understood.
This morning I walk through a dream
of desperate men and gaunt women
lining up to knock on my doors
or calling out to me from
their beds of slippery dark.
I woke up to the words *this is not*
my empire   I did not release the orders to kill
children in countries I will never see.
I did not permit people to use the crosshairs
of guns to hunt down innocent men, women and
children. I was born in a time of war
to an empire that I never claimed as mine.
I move through the morning
like a sleep walker
in a dream of terrible consequence.
This is not my empire

Spring Ice

My grandmother leans into her words
holds my hands

across her kitchen table.
Together we are crossing spring ice

each footfall a perilous step.
There was a train, she slept on the floor

she was the only one pulled off.
She says I have her mother's eyes

her father's cheek bones
her shy forehead

filled with too many dreams.
Try to understand   It feels like yesterday

not enough years have passed
that someone can forget

I am listening to her story about a train
a girl who slept on the floor, guards with guns

slung across their chests.
Steam fills the kitchen

from black pots
on her stove.

The Field

When they came for me
it was always dark
They put a hood over my head

When they beat me
I could not see
their faces

I learned to disappear
in the field I carried
hidden in the bones
of my body

My fingers dug deep
into dirt
that rose up
as motes of dust

White moths darned air
above yellow grass

*Is the table
they strapped me to
still there?*

When they beat me
and called in more men
the ceiling opened
into sky
blessing the field
my body had become

I walked with my mother
hand in hand
the long road to market

combed dusky grasses
catching fireflies
in my hands

to light the dark
of my cell
hours later

It Was Winter

The taxi driver let us out
by the Hudson,
his sleeve was pushed up.
He showed us numbers
tattooed there by the Russians.
He waited until we were
out of the taxi before he flashed
his arm out the window,
held it lifted, his hand in a fist
sleeve pushed up past
the elbow and said *look*
at these numbers
the Russians did that.
It was winter, the Hudson
was frozen in places, even the air
was frozen. We didn't speak
about the shape of ink tattooed
in that straight line on the soft
part of his arm, but we understood
how skin carries the history
of a life, sometimes wakes a body
from sleep, has conversations
with the dead and the living,
whispers greetings
every morning and tucks
you into bed at night,
offers reminders in the shape
of slanted numerals
you gently touch with one finger
lifting memories in rusty buckets
from that deep well
hidden inside your body.
We understood how numbers tattooed on an arm
become a mute language, dark bell,
living talisman.
He waited until we were standing outside

stamping the ground to keep warm
so there would be no
conversation
about those numbers
and what they meant in his life.

Dreaming Los Alamos

I open the windows to rain
next to my mother's bed
open myself to her
room of potted cactus,
paintings of wind swept plains,
frozen moon of her face
drifting in pillows.
Night keeps asking me
to braid her hair
before releasing me
from the dream she
wants to share
wandering in a desert
of female names
Circe, Persephone,
Bathsheba
lost daughters
seeking reconciliation
with the dead.
Skeletons rush past me
dragging whip-stitched
skirts,
sun burned features,
eardrums bursting with
explosions
beyond thee, inside thee,
on top of thee, below thee.
In this landscape everything
becomes biblical,
a prophecy of brimstone
or meal of ash,
this is Los Alamos,
this is the day of the dead.
My mother dreams of test sites
with features of
liquid mercury,

confuses death
with a beautiful dance,
foxtrots with the taste
of black water trapped
against her tongue.
Night looked like day
she whispers in my ear
when I bend to ice her lips.

My mother is dreaming
Los Alamos,
illuminating all the lives
stretched out below,
animal, mineral or vegetable,
each one blessed by
a fusion of dark petals,
this fiery thunderstorm
blowing black rain
across the face
of the world.

Living in a Mapless World

You say all that is now solid
will melt away.

See how birds disappear
into the horizon of history?

Where does the physical text
of one body end, your finger asks
moving against my skin.

They told us to crawl beneath our desks,
that we would be safe, this is how we would survive.

Now I am a woman claiming the landscape of
memory, the territory of desire,

the myth of her own survival in a land of plenty.
There is no compass for this kind of travel.

It is the end of some year and I sit at the edge of the world,
I lean against the heartbeat, I carry the curled bodies

of children seeking survival beneath their desks
in basements or dark tunnels.

Where does the physical text end
and the real world begin?

This morning I could not remember my dream.
Something about monks around a table.

My sister was there, then everything was gone.
That was all it was. One moment we were together,

I could feel the sense of longing,
then everything was gone

Where are we in this equation?

We have stepped over the edge of the known world.

We are free falling with no parachutes
the year is ending.

We are walking in the dark with no light
one step at a time

We are crawling out from beneath
our desks.

Gilgamesh Muses on Achilles' Heel, Time, War, and Life in General*

All morning I was thinking about your wounded foot
how you would trail a legacy of not only a pierced heel
but that you would pass on time's arrows to the rest of us.

I sometimes think my idea of trapping Enkidu's spirit
in a statue was all for naught, as time does fly, time does wound
each of us with her perfectly aimed arrows.

Your heel is not the root cause of suffering, Achilles,
and certainly did not force anyone to march off to war
against women and children, although after that last monstrous

battle in the Gulf, thousands of Iraqi children are dying the slow
        death
cancer from plutonium is most fond of, proving that
along with the decay of our mortal flesh, there trails behind us

that shadow of violence that is continually trying to re-knit itself
to our bodies. But as decay of the physical precedes our own human
        demise
so decay of the spirit is a precursor to decline of the planet.

Let's not lose sight of those great calves of ice that are thwacking
        themselves
into the sea even as you read this, and never forget the image
of polar bears swimming for miles to find a piece of solid ice and
        failing that

sinking into the arctic waters because, Achilles, as the bears drown so
        do we.
But the strange part of all this, the missing link so to speak,
is the beauty in the earth that surprises us when we least expect,

___

* *Gilgamesh was the fifth King of Uruk, modern day Iraq, circa 2,500 BC*

the color of wild orchids in the spring.
Lately I see our lives as a beautiful script that encompasses
everything that was, if only we could deal with that shadow

that keeps urging us to war. Everything we have wrought
can be undone in the time it takes to notice those orchids
and embrace those children.

Once in Luxembourg

Once in Luxembourg
death entered my room dressed like a working man.
Sleeves rolled up, shoes caked with mud,
smelling like stale beer, he stumbled
through my door by mistake but once there
he did not want to go. That was a hard night
spent talking over matters of the hereafter
versus living in the now and the next morning
I caught a plane
wearing a necklace of bruises around my throat,
a gift to remember him by. Years later we met again
when death whispered in my ear and lay down with me
like a lover anxious to please, holding
my entire body in her arms. Death had become a woman
who knew every secret pore of my being.
She glided inside my house of sleep
and waited for me all through the hot summer days
filled with locusts and the smell of pecans until
evening pulled night down in her lap and she could rise up
from inside my body, holding her arms out to me.
I learned to count the beats of her heart. I learned
to recognize her smell, quince and lemon.
I learned to welcome her touch. Nights we sat
on the porch under the redwoods and the dog
sat with us. The sky was salted with stars.
I taught her the names for things I loved,
obsidian and flint, mahogany and turquoise,
chalcedony and ambergris, things of the mineral world
immutable with the touch of wind or rain.
She moved like a ghost at the edges of my dream
down the long hallways of my past.
She wanted to become me and I wanted to
hold on to some boundary where earth throws down
her green arms and says only the living shall enter
here. Those were slow days but filled with
radiance as though everything I could be
was being shown to me, endless, a wide starry sky,
fields blooming with possibility.

The Widow's Chant

This is my husband's funeral pyre.
I step into the smoke to taste my new life of ash.

This is the morning my head is shaved, tendrils of hair
drift like a language of loss in front of my face.

This is the afternoon I am pushed into the courtyard
of my fears   O *brave and surrendered heart*

where all my saris the colors of gemstones
are taken from me and I am wrapped in white
the color India's widows may wear.

Nights I carry the memory of my other life
kneeling in the streets of my belly

when I was once a wife, mother, sister or daughter.
Here even the moon is shamed by the actions of men.

I carry the mantra of forgotten women
forming a dialect of the dispossessed

and wear the tattoos of my husband's life
hennaed on my palms and feet.

Thrown out of my husband's house I am part ebb and flow
through the streets of the night.

Some say to give thanks I am the embodiment
of his life and now I am living sati

no longer burned on the funeral pyre
with his body.

Listen to me repeating the soft syllables to this chant
in the city of widows where I make my home,

part of the long line of female ancestors
threading their way in and out of my life.

The Dead Girl Speaks

I did not know the dead could speak. I thought their houses
were dark windows with doors nailed shut.

I did not know my voice would fly out of the bones
of my chest like a wounded bird embraces flight.

But this is how the dead heal themselves into *mandalas,*
great fiery wheels filled with their stories, humming and whirling

through space. This is how the dead speak to the living
and the living must bear the weight that drifts down

that falls against their upturned faces as ash.
I did not know my voice would come out of me

in the shape of a bird, white crane, lifting off from all the ponds
of the world at once, stretching out into the one clear syllable

of my life. I did not know the voices of the dead grow stronger
as each year passes. Sometimes I hold hands with other dead,

we drift across the universal arch as one thought. We have become
an arrow of light. We are on fire when we penetrate the dreams

of the living. It is the sound of our hands brushing against their
        windows
that wakes them at first and then it is the sound of voices bearing
        witness

urging them to get up, get out of bed, listen to the stories
the dead have come to share, that settles like a rainbow-colored
        shawl

drifting against their hair, falling around their shoulders
brushing against their hearts.

Finding Solace

Recipe for Peace

Bare your feet, roll up your sleeves
oil the immigrant's bowl.
Open the doors and windows of your house
invite in the neighbors, invite in strangers off the street.
Roll out the dough, add the spices for a good life,
cardamom and soul, cumin and tears.
Stir in sesame and sorrow, a dash of salt
pink as new hope.
Rub marjoram and thyme, lemon grass and holy basil
on your fingers and pat the dough.
Bless the table, bless the bread,
bless your hands and feet,
bless the neighbors and strangers
off the street.
Bake the bread for a century or more
on a moderate heat
under the olive trees in your backyard
or on the sun-filled stones of Syria,
in the white rocks of Beirut
or behind the walls of Jerusalem.
In the mountains of Afghanistan
and in the skyscrapers of New York
feast with all the migrant tongues
until your mouth understands
the taste of many different homes
and your belly is full so you fall asleep
cradled in the skirts of the world
curled in the lap of peace.

Gathering The Voices

Where do the dead go when they abandon the living,
become sparks flying up to burn themselves out as stars?
Become ravens wheeling through the trees in my backyard?
In fall the dead gather in the live oak
outside my kitchen window.

I wash dishes while they chirp and wheeze or squeal,
happy to be alive in the light leaves cast down.
Are the dead lonely? Away from the land of their birth,
missing the smell of earth or sidewalks in rain?
Does nostalgia for the lost remnants of life
compel them to journey towards us?

Sometimes they cross great plains of ice or raft
torrential rivers to reach us. They arrive with a scent
of sesame, bearing gifts of sweet halva or baskets of spiced pears.
If I am lucky they bring bottles of fragrant *Noix de Saint Jean*,

red wine made from green walnuts, *eau de vie*
and sugar. I sit back and drink to them, to their passing,
to their families left behind, to the fractured nature of this world
or the mysteries of their world.

Sometimes they have learned a new language and they arrive
speaking in the colors of the desert, each color
demanding attention. Black is where everything begins,
language moves out from there into whispers of white, yellow or blue.

It is tricky learning how to communicate with them when they show up
speaking Aramaic and you still live on the north side of Houston
where not one living soul speaks that tongue. But the dead
carry their desire to be reunited like a burning bush,

impossible to turn away from, words coming toward the living
like flames from the bodies of saints filled with sentient knowledge
burning blue and white, ash from the vowels of their longing
falling like a rainstorm in your heart.

Bringing Me Back

The evening of the first surgery
my sister stood on one side of me,
my husband, sentinel-like, on the other.

Together we left the hospital
into the mysterious blue
of San Francisco's dusk.

The slow motion of drugs inside my body
caused me to smile at simple things,
helicopter blades, bumps in the sidewalk,
the undone frizz of my hair
in damp coast air.

Everything a mystery,
my body, the light, my sister,
my husband handing me pink and white lilies
so much perfume cradled
in the pelvic purse
of my lap.

Everywhere the mystery of pain or love
or simply how hands of male nurses
are filled with too much tenderness
to bear.

At this hour birds flock together
in all the cathedrals of trees.
The great golden bridge is filled
with families pushing strollers,
walking dogs, bicycling, roller skating,
all etched in Prussian blue.

I closed my eyes
leaned back
let both of them guard my body
let both of them bring me back.

We Show Each Other Our Scars

We show each other our scars, *think* Krakow at dusk
winter in the yard, lights like globes of fire
trapped in distant buildings, heat bundled in hands.

Think the train through Yugoslavia, how the guards
pulled you off at a checkpoint, guns slung across their chests.
We show each other our scars, *think* the world as lover or
first love, first sex, the heat, the mouth. Years later
longing mistaken for thirst.

We show each other our scars, the clock hands move forward
in increments, time branded on our features, our features
precise mirrors of our mothers or grandmothers,
mine in babushka, overalls, hoeing in the garden,

yours more distant, a dream in quilted coats moving through
your yard. We show each other our scars, *think* distant lands
filled with the faces of rivers broken into pieces by fish
against our legs.

We are wading across with canvas packs on our backs.
We show each other our scars, the world may stop spinning
sometime in the future, may speak to us in a language
we finally understand but by then it will be too late.

Somewhere there are two women lifting their shirts saying
my scar is on my left breast just over my heart
small smudge, the surgeon left behind this one
shadow trace like eucalyptus leaves at dusk or

mine is on the right breast, hooked under and curving
like a pavilion rooftop, like a smiling moon
a gardenia leaf floating in the pond of my body
moonlight ripples my water.

We are standing in the world knee deep, chest deep
treading this flow that sounds like twigs breaking
against our windows.

Together the world is standing in us asking if we are ready
do we want more, what can we bear to carry
what can we leave behind?

River Tongue

The legs of herons
like twin shafts of light
hollow the sound
entering the throat.

From the tongues
of rivers
the sad speech
this pretty song

drifting in and out
of our lives
like stitches in a young girl's dress

holding the form
just inside.
Transparent this cloth
that covers a pale blue secret

this ancient speech
this river tongue

sheep sorrel and thistle,
Queen Anne's Lace and wild orchids,
one great blue heron
rising from the water like a spirit
part earth, part air.

We take our clothes off,
light moves her hands
across our bodies.
There is humming all around us.

The water is speaking in tongues
is saying she is a very old woman
but she has the heart of a girl
the breasts and thighs of a girl.

I walk in and she is speaking to my ankles
is whispering something urgent now
against my belly and chest.

Somewhere night is falling in cities
far away from here
on street corners and bars
night is falling

but all I see is the female shape of water
moving her endless river
against my arms and legs.

My hair is slicked back
like an otter
or strange blue bird

lifting from the surface of water
disappearing in the dark trees
overhead.

Dancing In The Dark

This morning I stood
leaning into the left behind sorrow
geese weave in falling air.

I saw our lives spread out like a puzzle
of the known and unknown world.
I stepped out from our House Of Rain

and wanted a vision to fill me.
I wanted to gather the scattered pieces
of my family's past and conjure a healing

that would lift our long dead from out
of their pockets of sleep
and give their lives a new meaning.

I wanted to untangle the knots
from all the limbs of that distant tree
and lift it into some kind of green forgiving.

The truth is, nights I lay in my child's bed
and listened to their voices
bleeding through the rooms of our house.

I heard the scratched out vowels
the God of Guns and the God of Drink
speak to those who listen.

All my eight-year-old prayers for a passage
from one dark night into some other wider
lighter place only left me thirsty

with a mouthful of copper pennies
and the taste of rust-red water
trickling across my throat.

Days our father drove the deaf and dumb roads
searching for work while stars cracked
lightning above his head

were mornings where grief swept our floors
anxious as a hungry ghost for more
of what we didn't have.

If I have to choose, I choose the day we stood
above Big River and made wishes on leaves
we dropped down to the mud-filled water.

I choose the night our aunt raced our uncle
to grab the gun they kept hidden,
only this time she found it first.

I choose all the lost threads of our family's fate
and like a voodoo curse I put the broken pieces
back together again into some new shape.

I hide it in a mason jar sealed with tape
and place it in my kitchen window so the
sun's light fills the glass with a new radiance

and calls my ancestors
from so far a place, they fall like heavy ravens
out of night's darkest pocket.

They come trailing prayer shawls made of dust and dreams
to sit at my table and break bread with the living,
where shadows slip unseen into my body so I am marked

with these lines of their passing
much as the earth is marked by the
thrust and pull of the moon.

I am guided by this rush of all their longing
to discover what it means to be human all over again.
If I have to choose, I choose the sound

of their bare feet dancing in the dark
on salt-spread floors
through all the rooms of my house.

Queen Of Wands

I stuck my hands in my mother's apron,
pulled up pictures of long dead babies
in her arms.

I stuck my hands in her apron,
felt the sting of asafetida on my tongue
a cure for cursing, a cure for flu,
a cure for stormy relations.

I stuck my hands in my mother's apron,
smelled her cedar chest opening,
found moth balls like globes of sugar
sprinkled across my uncle's navy uniform.

I pulled up pictures of the dead
resurrected color into faces
jumped off jumping-off places

Stuck my hands in past the wrists
up to the elbows, shoulders,
this is her collar bone ringing my neck.

I pulled her apron over my head
tied it in a bow across my belly
her pockets next to my pelvis.

I stuck my hands in, pulled out
river smells in her hair
cypress sap on her fingers.
I dusted my hands with flour

measured in salt, rolled out the dough
flattened out days, lifted up her first dates
in Baton Rouge, farm boys on the porch,

live crawfish in a bowl on her table.
I stuck my hands in her apron,
pulled out the *Queen of Wands*,
determined, strong,

oiled the immigrants' bowl,
covered the bread.

Learning How To Love The Fire

The boy juggling balls of fire
at the Larkspur Ferry said it was easy.
You had to focus on keeping the motion constant
and the only time he burned his hands
was when a tourist pushed him in the back
because, she said later, she thought the fire was fake.
The flames that leaped off his palms
threw my mind spinning into some other time
when offerings were burned on a regular basis
to sleepy-eyed gods so far away
no one knew how to reach them
besides killing innocent children
or spilling fire across the body
of a snow white ewe
so the air would crisp up
and the heavens could be appeased
with this small gesture
causing the gods to wake
and bend to the ragged tribes
that lived in such grief
scattered about their knees.
If the offering was favorably received
the gods would smile to release rain
from the corners of their lips
and crops would multiply
and explode with green.
But this was not that time.
This was the boy standing
in front of the line
waiting to step onto the Larkspur Ferry.
This was the one with scars on his palms
who said to me without taking his eyes off the flames,

you have to learn how to love the fire.

Sometimes I Pretend I Am Asleep

Just after the first light turns our bedroom
into a pale blue cocoon and I know you are awake too,
I pretend I am asleep.

I listen to you sighing as though something
has torn loose in the lining of your soul,
as though you are facing some great blackness,

a tidal wave of perfect nothing pulling you under
holding you captive on that fatal shore.
Then I feel the whole bed shake

as you fling your arms out wide to
pull me into your body close to the vulnerable part
that is your belly and I pretend to finally wake up

and move to your hair and skin and mouth
so we are planted deep in our earth before the
morning truly rises.

For a moment it is as though we have just met
shy with touches and looks, until you rise up out of our bed
and small things take on great dimension.

The tea you bring back to me is exotic in that way
food and drink become when eaten on top of bed sheets.
All of these first moments take root in me

so I remember much later, pretending to sleep,
knowing you will pull me into your life
your body spilling over me like a great river
sending me out into the day wet and gleaming.

Hand-Signs

The nurse said go home, do nothing,
allow your body to heal. I walked to the nearest
Greek Deli to buy dolmas. I wanted to allow my body
to become a foreign country where no one spoke
the language of my birth and village children would laugh
at all my mispronunciations. She said do nothing
and I wanted to become the island of Santorini,
my body made up of black sand, volcanic, that glitters
after dark and carries bits of garbage washed up
from ferries in a hurry to get back to Athens.
I would have settled for Mexico, become a morning in
Chapultepec Park, holding my trees painted white,
ghostly, from the ground up, holding lovers,
girls in short skirts, macho boys.
I could have settled for Mexico or Greece, it was really
a tossup. She said to allow my body, so I did,
allowed my body to imagine climbing the one hundred eighty steps
to the shrine outside Puebla at dawn, my sister by my side,
everything smoked, hazy, thick wax candle in my hand,
Black Madonna waiting.
I allowed breathless things to enter my chest,
extend a hand, begin to tango. Women with
asymmetrical haircuts and drawn on mustaches,
men with flies unbuttoned and cigarettes hanging,
barefoot gypsies and legless beggars on rolling planks
were all the same to me, dancing circle dances around my knees.
Once on a ferry from Athens I slept on a pile of blankets
with a boy from Sicily. We weren't lovers,
just friends sharing blankets under stars crossing the Aegean.
He said moon was trapped in my hair
with hand-signs. I allowed my body
to sway to the rhythm of waves
remembering that ferry to Santorini. How easy
to trap moon in hair with hand-signs, the
way stars looked like slivers of needles
stitching sky up.

Everything I Know About Beauty

Everything I know about the human body
I learned in a subway car at 3 a.m.
when thighs and shoulders bump
unexpectedly into the other place that

shoots electric impulses from a hidden pool
at the bottom of my belly
I like to refer to as my LaBrea Tar Pit

filled with fossils of wrecked relationships,
flaming trolley cars,
deathly stings from innocuous looking
creatures, Yousef's dark eyes,

Marion's red lips   *are you getting this?*
plane crashes, terrorist attacks, lost loves,
tsunamis and mudslides, fires and plagues,
the inviolate becoming violated,
in that famous tar pit of my celestial insides.

On the subway
a gasp here, a shudder there
radiating signals up and down
my spine
tender and hopeful as the bodies of
construction workers unwrapping
egg salad sandwiches

one hundred stories high
or the fevered imaginations of men
stuck on the ground cleaning sewers
lounging around manhole covers
like guards to the underworld
whistling and calling at girls who pass by
in those tiny and tender
windblown skirts.

Nostalgia For The Rain

It began with a tin roof
sounds like silver sticks
falling from air
a dash of bird feet
despair or love at all the edges
It began with a car
gleaming bumpers
wind shield wipers forming a pattern
of lost and found
the truth of the seen versus
the unseen
It began with a picnic
wicker baskets of fruit
grass still dazed from a sudden
shower
It was spring
or was it fall
the brush of winter
woven into scarves
It arrived in the blue smell
at the base of clouds
became a dark thought
fell in torrents
released us from ourselves
It began with a mattress
on the cabin floor
the smell of wet pines
redwoods singing
in hidden groves
It came in a rush
unfolded wet knees
a vertebrae of desire
It began with your body
in the afternoon
the smell of rain
conjuring memories

silver sticks falling across
our shoulders
A dash of bird feet
on all the rooftops
of the world

Judith's Story

I am sitting on the porch
with my father.
I say *the cows are quiet now*
in all the dark barns.

He repeats the words slowly
not trusting his tongue
to release the correct sound.

Together we are creating
a poem to transcend
the land of Alzheimers
where my father dwells
in so many distant rooms.

I say *soon the sparrows*
will begin to build nests
and he follows my lead
word for word
lingering over *sparrows*

as though the form
and shape of a delicate spirit
has been set free
from it's body
and is a marvel of flight.

I say *our lives*
are no small thing
in this world
and he twirls a finger
as he repeats
no small thing.

I say *birds will begin*
to dream of the south
and he says *sparrows*
will build nests

I say *soon the sun*
will set
on this long day
and he says *so many sparrows*
in that tree and smiles

as though for one moment
he remembers
some other day
distant and hazed as an old watercolor

when I was a girl
and he was my father
closing the heavy barn doors
on all the quiet cows

and together
the two of us
walking back up the hill
hand in hand
passing beneath the tree

filled with the song of sparrows
that guarded our backyard.

Shelter Cove, Northern California

The moon not yet down
and light rising above redwoods
behind where we slept.

We came to say goodbye
for the last time
but fishermen were throwing nets into the sea
hauling finger-sized fish and we spent some time
watching their bodies dance above the waves.

Later I kept wanting to write in the sand
something about touching the mouth of another
human being for the first or last time.

That night, our bodies in separate sleeping bags
were *elemental* and *ancient*
and then before we fell asleep
became *awkward* and *elegant*

your shoulder blade beneath my finger
a curvature of flesh
that rises up to my hand,

your body always seeking
some short-cut to love.
Understand that this is only
a moment in time,

go slow. The way earth moves her plates
sometimes takes a lifetime,
water quickens under a full moon
there is always this backward glance up to that light
before the wave seeks sand

as in the way we are drawn to each other
last looks thrown over shoulders.

We will always meet in this
shorthand for braille
abbreviated moments of
slight touches.

How many words do I need
to describe this? *Bird, flight, lover, friend*
your body is releasing into my touch.

Untranslatable moon of you,
sweet slick of my awkward,
my shy reaching out to your body
my fingers read like a charm
one last time.

Reunion

I was dreaming about going home.
There were cattails barely moving
in pond water the color of rough emeralds,
the color of old light trapped
between the edges of the known world
and the other side where everything waits
to be named.

My father was part of this dream
repairing his roof with hot tar,
his hands kept lifting smoking buckets
like a character trapped in Dante's mind
he could never leave that rooftop
would never be released from hauling
flaming buckets to mend holes
that could never be mended.

I heard the woman next door calling her daughter
to come back in from all that darkness
as though she was Persephone
disappeared into that dark underworld.

I was dreaming about going home
where the lost are found and the silence
of recognition filters down.
I am always searching for this place
the chiaroscuro of my fate
layer upon layer of paint
I keep working my way through,
acolyte of the deceased
archeologist of the soul

this meeting place I am drawn to
grafted onto skin and bone.
Now and then a face surfaces, glittery with minerals
dug out of earth, mica or quartz
illuminating eyebrows or mouth.
Sometimes a voice leaks out calling like
the woman next door, frantic to be found
and released back into my world again.

Fly Fishing After Dark

In the photograph he is smiling.
His hands are the size of small shovels.
He was a fisherman who turned to farming
late in life,

a hunter who taught his sons
to love guns and then put down
his own rifles forever.

In the photograph there is a hint
of something complex, untouchable,
a remote land he is trapped in,
a blur of wind and rain filled with the last light

twilight brings, the underside of evening
opening up into dreams of rivers
threading blue stitches in earth.

My father returns to visit me
in the taste of loamy dark,
his figure rising up,
fly fishing after dark.

Swimming Home

When I call home the care-giver answers
and when I ask for you
I hear her say, "try to say something to your daughter"
then fumble the receiver against your mouth
so I can listen to your new language
of silence.

I am the wind in this conversation
moving restless in the limbs and leaves
of some great mother tree
trying to navigate miles of telephone line
with my voice strung out on the backs of mountains
or stalled with heat in some pale desert town.

I could say I am a rain forest
and you are that elusive rare bird
on the endangered species list
flitting around inside my foliage
your glossy wings appearing and disappearing
but always out of reach.

I woke this morning with the smell of the Bay
trapped in my head,
mosquito bites on my face, catfish cuts
on my hands.
Or were they your hands?
Was I in your dream, Mother?
skin glistening with salt, a child again
fumbling for speech?

I was treading water all day
my legs entwined with yours
your fingers smoothing my hair
my arm around your waist,
"try to say something"
became the mantra of our moment,

huge, relentless
this pressure on the heart
to force the tongue
to speak.

I swam all day
just to get out of the Houston ship channel
kick-free of sting rays and oil slicks
reach the wide opening of the Gulf.

As I swam I resurrected words
that defined who you were
okra gumbo on your table
fried catfish in black skillets
on the stove.

I repeated your secret recipes
sharing your prized words
until I became the living embodiment,
the archeology of you.

I swam in measured strokes
into the deepest recesses of our past
until I found your secret cove and climbed out
on the beach where you sat smiling
in your strapless black spandex,
mounds of sand dollars like flowers
scattered at your feet.

This is my path home
diving into our shared life
as though it is a famous wreck
covered by miles of the gorgeous
blue sea and now and then a shaft of light
opens up one of the drowned rooms

shines on forgotten photographs or
bone china plates, translucent in their
fragility, patiently waiting for their delicate
patterns to be rediscovered
and tenderly carried
to the surface of our lives
by bodies floating
in all the blue.

Moon, Boat, Water

At night she says my father comes to her.
She does not think this is a dream because
he is smiling and bends over her body
and that is when she rises up to greet him
but by then he is gone.

Sometimes there is the smell of the Bay
and she swears he has been there
home from a weekend in the Gulf.
Just imagine this, she says to me
there were no fish for me to clean
he has cleaned them already,
and the night is warm and still,
moon like a porcelain boat
trapped in the tree outside her window.

Sometimes she says he comes as though
he has stepped out of the Book of Water.
He is luminous with fire that dances
on the surface of his body.
There is a river between them
and he is calling for her to cross over.

She wants to go but there is no bridge
and while she searches
frantic to make her way to him
he slowly turns and disappears.

This time there is the smell of flowers,
white scent of magnolias or gardenias
drifting like small waves
trailing behind him.

Cassiopeia

My mother is sleeping in her chair,
the television her only companion.

She is dreaming about light rising on the waters of the Gulf
pulling fishermen from sleep and casting down shadows

of human lives on the ocean's floor.
She is dreaming the map of   *How*

on warm summer nights her children slept
on both sides of her in the yard

under some favorite aunt's quilt,
a gathering of vines and stories embroidered

in cotton with stitches too small to see.
Above them the night sky

whirled with fantastic shapes,
syllables of Gods or Demons

ricocheting in their webbing of black
with names like Orion's Belt, Dog-Star, or Cassiopeia.

There are no words now in my mother's sleep,
no consonants of debt or worry.

There is only the stillness of the summer evening
and now and then one bright star

burning itself out
in the firmament above her.

Learning Algebra

Some nights after making love
we roll away from each other
knowing it is almost impossible to bear
the power of one doubling the other
causing us to grow by tenths and hundredths
our bodies slick with this new formula.
The texture is pure algebra,
parallel line and perpendicular form.
This thrust, touch, lick and suck
all adding up to its equal.
My head is filled with this sorting and filing,
this convex and concave truth.
These signs are exotic
curled up that way inside our mouths.
The sentences we keep trying to form
keep coming unraveled
until all we can manage is for one
to pull the other into the flesh and blood
sum of this multiplication table.
The weight of our numbers is too dense
to allow room for speech.
Instead you offer your back
the length and curve of your vertebrae
that stretches out beneath my palm
speaks volumes to my hand.
I count the rings of bone with my fingers
while in the house a few yards away
the one light that still burns
belongs to my daughter.
Doing her algebra she struggles
numeral by numeral while we work out
the theorem of truth
that flesh equation that equals the two of us
forming our own parenthesis
here in mid-winter dark.

Cranes

What if we could pull back
every lost opportunity

every loss becoming a white bird
we cradle in our bodies

so we become receptacles
of transformation.

Imagine a field
cranes returning
to nest

and we are the light
they are flying
into.

A Brief History of Ink

Above the vineyards at dusk
we open the windows to greet the rain.

You show me the tattoo, 103 pinpricks of ink
forming Rings of Saturn at the base of your spine.

These lines of indigo married to black
undulate the surface of your skin

forming a certain shade of blue
created thousands of years ago with soot and oil

thickened with gelatin from animal skins and musk.
All this to realize themselves as a sign or a spell or a story

of rings in the imagination of a planet.

We lay down to greet the rain
and I say this is our

night in the Chinese garden of senses
when fingers once held solid cakes of ink

and shaved translucent pieces
in small bowls to melt into a substance

that would not smear
with finger pressure and so

performed the tender act of calligraphy
with a mercy of brushed or bamboo pens

whispering life into the alizarin heart, indigo mouth
pokeberry or cochineal mind of ink.

Somewhere I read they resurrected the mummy of an ice-man
whose body was tattooed with horizontal and vertical lines

at fifty-seven pressure points from head to toe and inside
the joints of his arms and legs

creating a healing map for acupuncture
tattooed thousands of years ago
when fire was a saving grace and ink

the mystical property of shamans
grown tired of caves.

Perched above the Napa Valley, I trace the rings of Saturn
at the base of your spine with just enough finger pressure

to resurrect Egyptian nights, block printing in China,
medicinal spells and ritual incantations

with the illumination, the astonishment
of ink in all her exotic transmutations.

I say the vineyards are on fire with moon
then trace the rings that guard your body.

Our gutters are gorged with this requiem
for water,

your story merging in the mind of Saturn
written in sworls at the base of your vertebrae

City Dreams

We go for coffee in the street
where goodbyes don't exist.
Boys wear hearts on their sleeves
alleys lead to piles of
nutmeg or coriander.

The city shakes out her skirts
opens her blouse, light traces
patterns that lead to her heart.
We go for coffee and receive magical spells
carved on cedar-screens
guarding the history
of her body.

The city holds us
in the crook of her arm
rocks us to sleep.
Morning opens
like a Chinese fan
white cranes in the folds
lacquered handle in our hands.

We go for coffee at the Fondouk
and become the smallest charms
dangling from the hem
of the universe
red skirts twirling
fingers snapping
moon clamoring for more
just above our heads.

Finding Solace

Walking across the Brooklyn Bridge we are a pair of feet
with hundreds of others finding solace in wind and air

hand in hand with migrant thoughts, how we all came to be sharing
space
in this country, this city, this bridge.

On a bus in Oaxaca we shared seats with chickens and rosaries, one
black goat,
kittens finding solace in the arms of children.

In the Dustbowl people found solace in wet sheets hanging against
cracks
filtering out sand fine enough to eat

until the sheets turned to mud and the sand caused dust pneumonia.
Sometimes solace blew through the air in the shape of tumbleweeds,

'Russian thistle,' they learned to eat until their throats were scratched
with too many memories of left behind homes and faces.

We are walking across the air of the city breathing in
junkie mornings and nights spent sandwiched in lonely bars,

elbows grazing strangers, glances given, numbers passed
on soft cocktail napkins to be bundled in your pocket

for the long ride home, breathless with the solace of anticipation.
Mornings in Rome I opened my windows to the jokes of garbage men

dressed in Baltic blue they jostled the cans and hugged each other
happy to have so much solace in the cast-off garbage of others.

I opened my windows to let their world in, remembering the morning
a long dead neighbor knocked on my door with bread and roses

"gifts for the living" he said, *solace* that lasted a lifetime
in the smell of flowers and in the taste of bread.

The Taste of Rivers

Open your mouth
I will pour the taste of rivers
into you

Navarro, Albion, Big River, Little Salmon Creek

The sand you taste
between your teeth

is the after-taste of river time
crossing and re-crossing paths

like lifelines you cradle
in the palm of your hand

The Albion tastes like moonlight
and cattails

The Navarro tastes like
wild sorrel and pine

Big River and Little Salmon Creek
taste like huckleberries eaten at dawn

If you fall asleep by the side of a river
you become part of the ebb and flow

from earth's great aorta
and share the dreams of salmon

swimming home
through the blue-chambered heart
of this land.

Black Phoebe

This morning waking alone in the cabin
the blue gray arms of sky just above
the bending trees pulling me up out of bed
to stand at the window, bare feet planted
on bare boards praying without knowing I was
praying for all the living we have left to do
and somewhere the song of one bird someone
named Black Phoebe etched itself in a simple
line against the breaks in my heart and I whispered
this is a good morning for birds and bare feet
and for all the living we have left to accomplish
even though time is such a reckless car flaming
us always toward such unexpected dips and turns
but standing like this planted in the morning
I felt that familiar voice grass and yellow
fields speak in, calling me to go outside
and walk to the barn and from there
follow the path that leads with her face
of such indeterminate longing
all the way to the sea.

Things Lost in Translation

Tell me something I haven't heard before.
How bridges in Paris are rusting bolt by bolt
and rivers are tired of their secrets.
How night loves to wash your body.

Empty the words from your pockets
rearrange stars if you have to
but tell me something untold before.

How your desire never sleeps.
How your heart shatters like glass
when you break bread with your father.

Tell me how you invite transgressions
and slip knots around the waist of afternoon
so twilight never leaves your side.

Weave syllables into a net that stretches
from the flea market on the outskirts of this city
all the way to the back alleys of your childhood

then speak to me in your native tongue
so I may grasp things lost in translation
and hold them like saltless tears
or small fires burning in wilderness.

Going Back To Selma With Rita

In the dream you're at the lunch counter again
pretending you don't see the way white men stare
up and down your twelve year old legs.
Outside the sky is trying to leak through the front window
where all your friends are waiting for you.

You keep thinking, that shade of blue,
trapped in white stares was the same color as your
mother's apron, not a true blue, but washed through
and through until the fabric was pale as paper
and just as thin.

Around one corner a smoking cross stands
dumbly quiet in your front dirt yard. You are a whisper
of brown in the sightless white fields
where cotton plants scratch a song against your legs,
those small sharp commas that you carry

stopping speech inside your head.
There is the distant sound of cicadas
pushing air between their wings
on the edges of the way you remember things.

The smell of burning houses pulls you out of this dream
to stand at the black windowsill of night
memorizing the way stars look like burning crosses
in the stillness of things.

Letter To Rumi

Dear Rumi,
I followed your advice
to take off my shoes
offer the soles of my feet
to the universal belly
walk to the river
just to hear
the ovation of the moon.

You were right
about the struggle to be slow and good.
I am trying to remember the path
that brought me
so many fragrant kisses.

I want to unhitch my sash
from this circle,
sit for a moment in quiet aloneness,
become the animal mind
that has the power
to change fear into solace.

Let it all enter me now
as an avalanche of fire
so I may pass on the words
to whoever waits
on the other side of this gate.

I am anxious to slip the vowels
into the warming place,
prepare for sleep
fold down the green bed.

Ten Aspects Of The World Without War

This is the morning soldiers dismantle guns
and abandoned tanks become nesting grounds
for cranes and starlings

This is the morning trees are planted in the ruins
of village streets and bunkers become seed exchange stations.

This is the morning that prayer flags fly
from the highest buildings in cities
that ring the world with chants or songs

This is the morning that snipers learn
the ancient recipes for baking bread
and distribute their loaves for free

This is the morning long tables are set
in the middle of rubble-strewn fields
where musicians gather to welcome everyone

This is the night where stars are recognized
in the deepest recesses of space
as a saving grace

and men, women and children
drift into sleep where there are no longer
the faces of war, but only the sound of wind
in trees or water forming waves
against some distant
shore

A Certain Kind Of Music

In the waiting room
I am surrounded by women
in thin cotton gowns
as though we all belong
to the same tribe

This day couples are walking
hipbone to hipbone
across the lacey architecture
of the Golden Gate Bridge

Nazia offers me her hand
I was born in Syria, she says
Roll on your right side
and open your gown
above your heart

I used to cry myself to sleep
thinking about my family
left behind
I used to jump at every loud sound
My dreams smelled of smoke

This day couples are kissing
on a bridge the color of sunrise
Trees are raining yellow thoughts
on all the sidewalks of the world

Lift your left arm behind your head, please

There is the smell of smoke in Nazia's hair
Birds are beating dusk into air
My heart is filled with
a certain kind of music

Letters From The New World

out of the bones of earth

I could say out of the bones of earth
a new world will rise beyond our wildest dreams
a new beginning of salt marsh and bird wing
or mountain face and pool holding moon reflection

I could say out of the chaos
there will be an unfolding as in petal by petal
the planet will unwrap her body until only
some bright essence is left

I could say this is the place that will call us back
wildly singing into the heartbeat again
so the long lines of despair and ancient face of war
melt away into the wide open palms
of men, women and children

I could say O green crying
blue singing
dark radiance shattering the ordinary into extraordinary
this sphere of our turning chant-like
spirit infused and brought back
to ourselves again

I could say the bones of earth
are all we have left
this estuary of our minds, cartography of our lives
pure seed naming us as hers
pulling us forth into and beyond the known world

I could say the bones of earth
hold the unclaimed, unloved, discarded language
of all our lives as one life
they have your face and mine
each bone a map of desire, structure of broken promises
now mended, desert and radiated universe healed

I could say the dust I throw out from my hand today
or take into my mouth tomorrow
is the hopeful archangel of a new morning
rising up off bent knees
reaching out, grabbing hold of us as a beacon,
icon, evidence or prayer, howl or sound of bare feet

pounding songs into the ground
creating a dance that comes from meeting the one love
of our lives and falling into the spell sex weaves
with life, birth embroiders with death
I could say begin here, out of the bones of earth
everything is possible.

Barcelona Beatitudes

Bless me black water and dogs of the night
woman with red dress and bare feet
moon drunk on the smell of spice and fire.
Bless me streets not of my birth but of my desire,
lost brothers and doomed sisters,
children with cardboard homes.
Bless me angels with no wings,
bodies held in secret embraces
alleyways and underground fears.
Bless me sun rising in the sex of my life,
Satan before you were Satan,
girls with lipstick mouths.
Bless me torn love, empty dreams,
stars, wind and rain,
morning afters and nights before.
Bless me cathedrals with doomed features
fingertip by fingertip
filled with rosaries for the dying
or buried with the dead.
Bless me cars and smoke,
the rush, the fall of life,
stockings in ruins,
flamenco mouth.
Bless me where this dance begins
with my head thrown back
holding the ears of night
mouth of morning
arms wide open,
my naked body
my ripped soul.
Bless me Barcelona
in the twilight of my passing
morning of my re-birth
evening of my life
wide open room of my heart.

Letters From The New World

The sun is sliding around to the other side
curving under the ocean, sinking west.
Everything here is in retrograde.

If we try to follow that path, curving beneath our feet,
light swaddling foreign places,

we come up in the animal market in China,
skunks in lonely cages, squirrels and snakes

food for the masses with a retrograde taste.
You are buying rattlesnake in alcohol

her beautifully preserved body, sliding scales
still vibrant beyond life.

Monsoon rains in India pull the sun past
surprised faces of holy cows or bounce in splinters

off the bodies in sequined saris
stacked on funeral pyres.

We are in Syria, land of your birth
the moon is in a tail spin, the sun is ahead of us

illuminating the hard boiled egg, the dates,
the Syrian coffee your hand is lifting in a small blue plate.

Mercury is still retrograde, painting abstract oils of everything.
This is you, now it's me, our breaths mingle

in the air we breathe. How did everything become so separate
so apart? When did we forget to remember our parts?

You interviewed your aunt in Tel Aviv   *I am still a survivor,*
Write my words down

The same way a taxi driver in New York
once showed me numbers, lifted his sleeve in silence,

pointed to the tattoos on his arm. Was this done by the Germans
or the Russians or was it done by us?

My mind is spinning, writing SURVIVOR in capital letters.
When did everything become a battleground?

We are following the sun from a beach in Northern California
where whales have begun to wash up, slipping bodies filled with blue
        songs

out of the water under cover of night so there is no savior in sight.
This is Lebanon after the bombing.

You talk as though life has always been this great sinking,
this retrograde flight, the breastbone curving backwards

into the long history of our nights. They are eating fish
in Iraq, still fishing in the Tigris. The sun is pink and gorgeous

falling into a nightmare flight through the smoke of bombs
but full moons here are renowned, blood red in the evening

filled with a million particles of us, our footprints in space,
the ones we leave behind for those who follow

seeking answers to all the questions of *Who were they? What went wrong?*
Here are whale bones, and shards of blue Syrian plates

here skeletons of many small animals
in what once may have been a market place or

was it one of their sacred sites? Were these the remains
of some strange religion?

Is this how they made offerings to a distant God?
Is this the way their people prayed?

When Cortes Burned The Aviaries

There had to be a price we were all doomed to pay
for that bit of arson,

screams of great blue herons flying up to escape
so much smoke, the smell of burning feathers,

emeralds, blues, molten reds, pink seashell, skyshell,
shellacked colors of those wings,

endless ideas of escape, drifting back down
into the arms of flame and the eyes of Cortes watching.

That afternoon I was so hot I tried freezing watermelons
but it made them soft as pink sponge.

I pulled my hair into a washerwoman knot,
knot of good faith, Cape of Good Hope came to mind.

I wanted to be sailing away from such fiery thoughts
but sat immobilized by heat

directly under the fan and thought instead of Cortes
burning the aviaries,

the march for gold, the rise of madness, heat spiraling away
from my body like a flock of burning birds,

each one stopping to look me in the eye
and sing out their name

white egret, vermilion flycatcher,
blue-throated hummingbird

all their ghosts flew through me,
condors, green jays, summer tanager

until the sun finally sank behind the far hill
and I could pull the curtains

covering my windows open again.

If I had been at sea on a ship trapped in the doldrums
it would not only be

a matter of having a sextant to determine latitude and longitude
I would also have to see and feel my body

as a presence in the world with incredible accuracy.

But I was landlocked and could only sit beneath a fan
hair knotted

and muse on the machinations of men burning birds,
then women and children, that most beautiful city of Tenochtilan

scratched out.

Once my sister took me to visit the ruins,
we stood beneath the pyramid of the Moon Goddess.

It was my birthday, heat crackled the air
sky was electric with blue

and not one bird in sight
anywhere.

Self Portrait By Frida Kahlo

Dear Diego,
What more can I say? I think our moment
is trapped in the smell of dust and holy water,
the thrust of paint brushes licking color into air,
the way midnight stings your body into believing light
will never come and you are happy to fall into any dark lie
that whispers in your ear.

Diego, I think we were destined for something more
than blank canvasses could hold. The sound of rain
reminds me of our bed in the dusk of afternoon,
yellow light turning red, falling like a bruise
on the floorboards of my heart.

Life was almost too much to bear, the way it came at me
with both fists, but I learned how to survive, opening up
all the closed doors of my soul so even the darkest recesses
fell under the spell of my paint brush, transforming my world
into self portraits with parrots or monkeys
as part of the spell.

Life is a dance step we are always trying to perfect,
love lost somewhere in the shades of red or found
in the sidelong glance of aquamarine.
If I say *the water gave me hope* and filled my body
with infinite possibilities, it is because I saw reflections of nature
drifting around me, undone from her skirts of loss
or her bindings of man-made fear.

When I paint skeletons sleeping above my bed
it is because I see the spirit that connects all our dreams
with wood, water, air, and fire.
This morning I wear a necklace of thorns
while I paint the love embrace of the universe
with the two of us in the lap of *Mother Mexico*.

I paint the *disintegration* of the physical as *a few small nips*
the universe has given to me. Self portraits are windows to my soul
filled with unimaginable hope and a few small birds
capable of soaring far above the wounded shape
my body holds.

If, Prophetess

According to prophecy there will be a great darkness.
We will be enveloped, our bones will turn to ash
even as we are fleeing. We will sink down to our knees.
We will find the earth again mid-waist as we are crumbling.

We will tongue the word, forgive. The sky will open,
there will be an ululation of spirits rising up. Cats will embrace mice,
crocodiles will offer tiny hands to us. They will pull us out of our fear
        of change.
Their tails will sweep a path for our passing. This is evolution.

If prophetesses are found pushing carts at Wal-Mart, we must
        recognize them.
They have come from the Lower Depths fresh from drinking bitter
        coffee
with Gorky. They have risen with mouths tasting of caffeine
in the blood and marrow of a technological vision. They are us.

Remember that flood? The Ark with seams swollen with salt, camels
        mating
in their awkward lovely fashion. *Great hooves buckling golden hips.*
The rhinos watching, anxious for darkness to slip a wedge of fan
over their sexual organs so they too might gallop the midnight steeds
        of ecstasy.

Remember the man with the nay-sayer name proclaiming "two by
        two" at the plank?
How he tossed the third one back. The abandoned ones swimming,
        slippery as kelp
frantic to get on board while the chosen couples watched those bodies
sink under turbulent waves.

Those were the good days, buckwheat in the hold, rye not yet
     poisoned with mold,
smell of osage orange, gardenia drifting. That boat has sailed, is not
     returning.
The rhinos have days and days of endless darkness to spread great
     vulvas open wide
to take in those strong yet delicate wands of good hope
to insure future generations are plentiful and multiply.

If prophetesses are us, we have risen out of such flooded regions,
those who once were cast off, who did not make the boat. We
     transmuted our bodies
into a new breed of fish.

Are you remembering this part? The gulp of water
filling the lungs with currents, those fins, the scales erupting,
propelling us into that millennial swim until finally the whssk-whssk-
     whssk
sound of trees near water that meant we were given a second chance.

The sprouting of legs, the climbing out, out. How fragile our chests,
little delicate cages
filled with such surprised hearts, red sparrows tweeting and tweeting.

How beautiful that first morning, pristine jewel of earth
welcoming us home again
The words that floated like blimps of technicolor
popping inside our ears.

"you are the way
     your body, the instrument
          take this yucca leaf
               eat, sleep, dream yourself
                    a new land"

Snake

I was the woman pulled out of Adam's side as a small sliver of bone
God named rib. Adam did not cry out when I appeared
only lifted his hand and offered me his mouth.
Snake told me later she/he saw it all, how God slipped
his hand in Adam's perfect flesh and without a thought
to his son's health broke the bone clean off. Snake winked
at that. I cried and covered my eyes. What is loss
in the face of such great shame?

There was jasmine growing wild, heavy scent
of honeysuckle and ropey vines of (should I whisper this next word?)
passion flowers. There was the smell of sex everywhere we went.
The air was stung with bees and white moths
shimmered against our skin. I could say it was not my fault,
blame it on the vibrant pattern of scales
that rose and fell each time snake climbed a tree
and hung her/his dazzling body just within sight
long enough to throw splinters of color igniting rainbows
against my skin.

I could say it was God's fault for creating such fragile
lives in such an abundant place. Later snake comforted me
in ways Adam never did. She/he listened and
encouraged me to speak my thoughts, helped me find my voice
so I felt a wide opening in my heart,
a singular plain of female knowledge
about to burst forth, a light that could not be contained
by one man or for that matter
by God's plan.

This is no confession, I knew what I was doing,
the acolyte of wind was drawing me to her,
muse of a larger understanding grown vast as a universe of stars.
I am Eve. I picked the fruit, kissed the snake
and welcomed the unknown world
waiting just beyond the garden's gate.

The Blue Mosque

I kneel with women
on our side of the Blue Mosque.

I wrap a black shawl
across my hair
here where the street
curves her questions

with no answers
and moon falls asleep
on the rooftops of the world.

I open my pores
to receive tears
the women share with me.

I swallow their vowels
of heartache and love
conceived by bodies
covered in veils.

I am filled
with the question
of eyes and hands
tattooed in red prayers.

I offer a hennaed blessing
painted on my palms
with red paste,
lemon and sugar.

I bend low
to enter the gateway
of new beginnings
where artifacts from lost lives

crumble to dust
beneath my knees.

Califa

California is a woman dreaming outside time
sleeping with her face to the sea, abalone shells
in her ears, chalcedony at her throat.

She holds feathers dipped in blood, repeats
the mantra of the sky at dusk. She dreams of great
fault lines. She dreams of pushing free

from the country that tries to contain her.
She carries a distant longing that moves through her
like a migration of wings envelops the sky.

She dreams of all her children scattered like seeds
that sprout inside her mouth. At dusk she slips
inside your bones to walk the streets of your hometown,

eat chili peppers out of paper cups, dance to La Bamba
in the parking lot of your backyard. She undoes her hair,
opens up her dress. She is not in mourning for all that is lost,

she is reclaiming what is hers with the party of old souls
stamping on trash cans and beating drums
in the living room of your grandmother's house.

She is a hungry ghost eating all the tortillas and beans
in your sister's kitchen, betting crazy stakes
with the Hell's Angels who live next door.

When night falls she slips back into the shape
of a crow to call out the names of places you forgot,
rising like a litany inside you   *Pacoima   Boyle Heights
Locke   Hunters Point   Crenshaw   Cucamonga.*

Rome

The first time was all about the land outside
the city, the way it slid inside us in shades
of orange, a fire-eater's dance with

a jug of gasoline and a wand to slip in your throat.
That kind of burning from the inside out
and we swallowed everything the land wanted to feed us.

We memorized the slant of each afternoon
as though it was a text of light mated to wind
and headed into the pelvis of the city.

Men kept wanting to be friends with you
because of all that wise silver trapped
in your hair and leaking out from the

soul of you, it was a Roman thing this
need to touch and pet sorrow or happiness,
unleash all the dogs of regret and make temples in

chests so bodies could be transformed into
walking prayers and the city could lie
back in anyone's arms morning, noon or night.

We were grafted out of pigeons and red stone,
out of espresso and gelato, out of the eyes
of all the workers bending to build a street

by laying down each round stone on their
hands and knees. It was ancient and prayerful
beyond modern and carried the scent of figs

mixed with the smell of cat in the Roman ruins
beneath our feet. We became the shadow
of every lover eclipsed by moon and water,

fed on dreams and wrapped in hair shirts,
spooned the long thin dances of branches
against our windows, slender as sticks of cinnamon.

We almost became a nun and monk
in our hurry to devour everything Roman
and at night we dreamed

the figures of marble statues could
slide their blue veined legs beneath our sheets,
loosen our tongues with tiny sweets

and entomb our bodies forever
with the mummified faces of popes
everyone loved but hated. Rome was

a ragged little sparrow that took
off in a wild heat and soared into
the sunlit rooms of our minds crowing

like a rooster until we slipped into the rhythm
of wine and cheese for breakfast, lunch and dinner
and stumbled across bridges that curved

their soft green arches like stammers
of speech above rivers that mumbled of love
or suicide but in the end could only save us.

Everywhere else the world was collapsing
but we kept climbing back up on ladders
made out of slip knots woven through

names like Ponte Vecchio,
Navona, Santa this or that, sculpted faces
of the Madonna or nuns with faces caught

in the grip of some ecstasy, portals
of lust we just collapsed into
until we became the softest feature

of any stone gargoyle we passed,
a tongue or earlobe, erasing our past
and in the heat of evenings we lay in all the city
parks split with light

and dark just to feel the
backside of Rome after night fell
in our laps.

Lunch With Adonis

We decided to meet one last time, invite Fortuna, Goddess
of the Wheel of Fortune, throw down the jackal's teeth

in the backwater alleys of our souls and sit down together
for a drink of my choice.

I thought it called for something archaic
with a hint of the modern gothic,

spider webs for instance, with an after-taste
of Cleopatra's breath, so I ordered milk of asp.

You were fashionably late, mosquitoes circled you
like a golden net, anxious to taste such beautiful blood

recently risen from Persephone's bed.
One last drink was all I could bear,

the rusted chalice of my despair so evident in the face
of your boyish beauty. One last drink, no foot stretching out

to embrace the muscle of my leg, no nipple-brushing eye stare.
I was the Insomniac Queen pulling her soft wedge of geese

as backup. You were the familiar road after dusk,
lion's lair with your bag of dragon's teeth. It was an omen

I missed, the scattering of the white bits across the barroom floor
could only have been a harbinger of grief.

I opened my body to the possibility of escape
while you pulled a stool closer so we were knee to knee

face to face. Oh Zeus! This was going to be hard!
I thought to call up my Scottish heritage

believing in the superiority of pillage and plunder,
I chastely mentioned the disgraced foe, Horse-Mouth,

but you remained unimpressed in your beatific pose.
I felt the old vortex opening and, lulled into your

charming perfect little teeth, I moved closer
to see if you had scars from possible recent
face work. But your skin was smooth as a baby's ass

and I was mesmerized as usual. I threw back my milk
and asked for something stronger, something that would flame

the throat and engage the heart, and then it was, the face
of your old rival surfaced, my lover, that old goat Fergus,

and I was quick to remind you how his penis was seven fingers
in length and his scrotum as big as a sack of flour, wondering out loud

if you, sweet boy, could match that? I caught a blink at size and
        proportion.
Our drink was coming to an end. This lunch now a night-time game

of truth or dare causing you to fidget with your designer jeans
and their crafty opening. "Let's call it a draw" I heard myself say,

smiling at my fortitude in the face of so much provocative flesh.
I threw down a golden slipknot only I knew how to open

and left you anxious for more repartee. "Same time next year" I
        called out
while my body shape-shifted from woman into eel, settling on raven,

back out the door.

Letter From The Seer To Odysseus
On Abandoning His Job as Hollywood Tour Guide

Odysseus,
You said the day you stood in front
of the tourist from Kansas City
and tried to explain the importance
of Mickey Rooney in the annals
of Hollywood lore, was the day
you decided to change your life forever.
You said you needed a journey to end
all journeys. You were bored or tired
of the routine you had fallen into and you
needed something to thrill you out of
your everyday senses. You longed for
the snap of sails, the gleam of bronze,
the arc and thrust of blades winnowing
air. In one word, you wanted
an odyssey. Not just your local drive-by
of all the famous haunts that make
Hollywood the land of rising stars and washed up
has-beens, you were sick
of describing the exploits of the famous
to the adoring masses from Kansas, Idaho
or Bouerne Falls. Go ahead and say it,
you were famished for naked flesh, minotaurs and
Sirens, Cyclops and years of bad breath.
As seer I have to say I have seen a thing or two
in your tea leaves and more than that in
the smoking guts that spilled out of that
sacrificial white deer but I suppose
it won't do me any good at this point
to warn you about that bewitching Queen
Aeaea or the sexy bed Circe loves to offer
available sun-burnt men. I'm envisioning
a strange ship with black sails headed to
some destination with the uninviting name
of The House of Death. I suggest you take

this ball of wax…it's soft enough to mold
into the shape of your inner ear and thwart
any bewitching songs certain sexy maidens like
to perform as a ruse to beguile and seduce
journey-crazed men. One more thing,
remember that no matter what happens
the journey is the thing, all your imagined feats
and lusty encounters are brief flames in
the galaxy of bonfires that illuminates
our spirits forever in the heavens so that
our brief moments become matters of
concern only when they truly touch the
heart of another. So journey on, Odysseus
(although I might have counseled you
not to give up your day job, I will offer
you my hand at this beginning place
on your path)…..It is truly your path,
so embrace the shape no matter where it
leads you….The universe awaits
your footfalls.

Sam's Story

The spring before I was born
my father drove the western edge
searching for work

like an arctic explorer
possessed by dazzling white
and the spirit that lives in ice

he was pulled beyond himself
by the dreams of others.
North wind at his back,

he aimed his car
toward some mythic
City of Angels

smelling of oranges
and light,
creating technicolor dreams

by shooting day for night.
He talked about those days
as though they were mantras

spilled from the mouths
of men and women
trapped in a dream

of finding fool's gold.
Picking raspberries
stained his fingers

the color of blood
until the land opened up
and he lay down

beneath the arms
of almond trees,
guarded by Orion's belt

and the wise teeth
of the Dog-Star.

Life is a jigsaw puzzle
he liked to say,
and fitting the pieces together

is a journey with no guarantees,
but he saved his roadmaps
as totems,

each crease and fold
marking the time
and place of his passing

when he was still a boy
and the land stretched out
before him

so he could play
all the riffs
of the western edge

like a tenor sax
blue notes scattering
like shooting stars

rising and falling
that spring
around the shape
of his car.

After-Life

You arrive exhausted, clutching your dog's leash
trailing bits and pieces of your former self.

A grocery list flutters from your back pocket,
scribbles of zucchinis and tomatoes, toilet paper and soap.

You arrive smelling of earthly expectations;
maybe you will win the lotto or be deeded that ranch

on the banks of the Llano. Bees and hummingbirds
herd the line forward. A woman walks behind you

her hair a flaming bush. She does not seem to mind flames
and pearly smoke. Gone is concern over things

you no longer have control over. Lanterns bob in the distance
like a painting on Chinese silk. Something is waiting to receive you

just as you are   dirt beneath your nails, leaves in your hair, a bit out
        of shape,
the taste of rock, a grit-filled reminder of how you fell out of earth

down a high canyon trail and ended up in this place. Your line moves
step by step into air the color of robins' eggs in spring.

Carrier pigeons, long extinct where you came from, cooing
        everywhere,
light coppery in a brilliant sheen you want to take hold of but

with a buzz and a prick, bees and hummingbirds those tiny guardians
of lost souls keep moving your line forward.

Pictures From Ellis Island

This is where he came through,
passing in a portal of dreams,
your grandfather, seventeen,

standing at the rail searching
the horizon for some sign
of the new life waiting just ahead.

His past quivers at his back,
echoes the brittle nature
of fields with no rain

or the stubborn release of stars
across the face of a sky
grown weary with war.

Like a fist of dark birds,
the way thoughts of home
explode inside him.

The cotton handkerchief he carries
wrapped around black bread
still smells of his mother's kitchen.

He stands at the threshold of the world,
spiraling thoughts of lost immigrants
gathering around him,

colliding with words he holds
beneath his tongue, practicing hello
or thank you in English,
preparing to greet
his new beginning.

Taxi To The Red Sea

I bought honey dates imported from Israel
and thought of my brother who journeyed
to Jerusalem as an artist on a famous dig.

He drew bones all day by the Red Sea,
sent me postcards smelling of dust and holy places
and wrote down curses he collected

that I read at work in front of my operator's board,
plugging in voices for the telephone company
until I was fired from that job.

No more long taxi rides from the city
to the suburbs with soulful taxi drivers
paid for by the telephone company.

Once a taxi driver asked me softly
if there was someplace we could go to talk.
It was a secret code for sex,
a certain sorrowful taxi driver kind of thing.
The moon was elliptical, was uneasy, was spilling fire
down the front of the taxi, orange flames everywhere I looked.

I used to dream of the Red Sea bursting into flame
my brother spitting out curses against the Evil Eye
trailing fire from his body.

In Athens I dropped my hand in a basket of stones
painted to look like eyes and came back up
with a fistful of good luck.

In Rome a man went crazy on our bus
#64, filled with priests and nuns, ran screaming
from one end to the next, frantic to get off.

Perhaps he was fleeing the Evil Eye
or searching for love in the shape
of moonlight torching a taxi.

Perhaps he was a taxi driver
Perhaps he was my brother
Perhaps he was myself.

Cartography In Blue

This morning I walked out of the city of my birth
as an immigrant in a land of immigrants

past homeless camps and coffee shops, neon faces of bars
and schools with razor wire fences, searching for that one place

the heart can find refuge in, moving as a migrant thought
filled with stories passed down from heart to hand to mouth

from the long line of ancestors stretching out behind me
wandering lost in the cartography of a time and place

undone by war and hate, famine or greed,
wandering like the *Rivers and Mountains Poet*, Hsieh Ling-yun

in a *place beyond knowing*.
Walking through the streets of our lost innocence

I welcomed home the mother tongue of all my brothers and sisters
with a thousand syllables for hope, a million dialects

for grief. I will oil the immigrants' bowl and make bread,
flatten out the days of our lives, roll out our stories,

cover the dough, let the bread rise, celebrate this recipe
in the subways of New York and the alleys of L.A.

I kneel next to the Red Sea in a land trapped between Africa and Asia
where white cranes feast on freedom in flight

and call down twin blessings of hands kneading dough
or words the air speaks

from tenement dreams to field songs, from the ceremony of cranes
lifting white wings above my face
to the sound of a tenor sax, perfect blue notes
free on any street corner of the world.

ACKNOWLEDGEMENTS

My immense gratitude to Robert Yoder, publisher of Wild Ocean
Press, for his continual faith in my work, and to Sharon Doubiago
for inspiration, friendship and shared poetry journeys over a lifetime.
A special thanks to the Helene Wurlitzer Foundation for a poetry
residency during which many of these poems were written and to all
the poets, artists and musicians whose works have sustained me during
the writing of this book including; Francisco Alarcon, Andrea
Clearfield, Lenny Foster, Cynthia Hogue, Susan Maeder, Pat
McCabe, Sangeeta Laura Biagi, Dottie Moore, Nancy Ryan, Ruby
Bell Sherpa, Nonny Ekedahl, Heidi Svoboda, Judith Brown and
Sheila Barcik. Many thanks to Theresa Whitehill and Paulo Ferreira
for use of their beautiful St. Helena studio. I am indebted to my
siblings for all their love and support along the way; D.J. Baker,
Suzanne Baker, Paloma Baker, Uli Thoma, Steven Baker and Melania
Kang. And, as always, love and gratitude to Barry, Ian, Greg and
Solange.